ASSESSING YOUR CHILD'S PROGRES

Testing and assessment in the National Curriculum

Pupils between the ages of 7 and 11 (Years 3–6) cover Key Stage 2 of the National Curriculum. In May of their final year of Key Stage 2 (Year 6) all pupils take written National Tests (commonly known as SATs) in the three most important subjects: English, Mathematics and Science. Your child may already have taken some National Tests at the end of Key Stage 1 (Year 2). These will have been in number, shape and space, reading, writing, handwriting and spelling.

At the end of Key Stage 1, your child will have been awarded a National Curriculum level for each subject tested. When your child eventually takes the Key Stage 2 tests, he or she again will be awarded a level. On average, pupils are expected to advance one level for every two years they are at school. The target for pupils at the end of Key Stage 1 is Level 2. By the end of Key Stage 2, four years later, the target is Level 4. The table below will show you how your child should progress.

	7 years	11 years	
Level 6		◼ (blue)	◼ (blue) Exceptional performance
Level 5		◼ (grey)	◼ (grey) Exceeded targets for age group
Level 4	◼ (blue)	◻ (light blue)	◻ (light blue) Achieved targets for age group
Level 3	◼ (grey)	◻	
Level 2	◻ (light blue)	◻	◻ (white) Working towards targets for age group
Level 1	◻	◻	

Assessing your child's progress throughout Key Stage 2 of the National Curriculum

The aim of the Letts Assessment books is to help you monitor your child's progress in English, Mathematics and Science throughout Key Stage 2. There are four books for each subject – one for each year, starting with 7–8 year olds. The questions in the books become progressively harder with each year, so that for 10–11 year olds, the questions will be at a level similar to the Key Stage 2 National Tests.

After completing a book, your child will have a score which you will be able to interpret using the progress indicator provided. This will give you a guide to the level at which your child is working.

i

ASSESSING YOUR CHILD'S PROGRESS

Using this book to assess your child's progress in Mathematics

This book is for 9–10 year olds (Year 5). It contains four basic features:

Questions: 42 questions, arranged in order of level of difficulty as follows:
                5   at Level 2 (pages 1–3)
                11 at Level 3 (pages 4–11)
                6   at Level 4 (pages 12–23)
                10 at Level 5 (pages 24–32)

Answers: showing acceptable responses and marks

Note to Parent: giving advice on what your child should be doing and how to help

Progress Chart: showing you how to interpret your child's marks to arrive at a level

- Your child should not attempt to do all the questions in the book in one go. Try setting ten questions at a time. If your child does not understand a question, you might want to explain it. Although the questions in this book are not meant to constitute a formal test, you should encourage your child to answer as many as possible without help. Read the questions to your child if you think it will help.

- When your child has completed the questions, turn to the Answer section at the back of the book. Using the recommended answers, award your child the appropriate mark or marks for each question. In the margin of each question page, there are small boxes. These are divided in half with the marks available for that question at the bottom, and a blank at the top for you to fill in your child's score.

- Collate your child's marks on the grid on page 46. Then add them up. Once you have the total, turn to page 33 at the front of the Answer section and look at the Progress Chart to determine your child's level.

- Work through the answers with your child, using the Note to Parent to help give advice, correct mistakes and explain problems.

Equipment your child will need for this book

The following equipment may be needed for answering these questions:

- a pen, pencil, rubber and coloured pencils

- a ruler (30 cm plastic ruler is most suitable)

- a calculator. An inexpensive four-function calculator is all that is required. Do not let your child use a scientific calculator which has too many complicated functions

- a mirror and tracing paper. These are useful for symmetry questions

- angle measurer. The angle measurer is probably easier to use than the protractor

Some questions in this book ban the use of a calculator.

The following symbol is used:

1 Jane said, "I know two addition sums that make 2:

$$0 + 2 = 2$$
$$1 + 1 = 2$$

and three addition sums that make 3:

$$0 + 3 = 3$$
$$1 + 2 = 3$$
$$1 + 1 + 1 = 3.$$"

> Can you write down **four** addition sums that make 4?

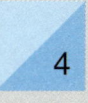

Q1

....

....

....

....

2 Some children bought comics at the school fair. Mary bought 3, Asif bought 7, Leone bought 5 and Peter bought 6.

a

> How many did they buy altogether?

Q2a

 ....

b

> If the comics were sold for 2p each, how much money did they spend altogether?

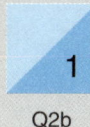

Q2b

....

MARKS

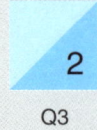

2

Q3

3

Fill in the missing numbers in these sequences.

a 31, 32, ☐, 34, 35, ☐, ☐

b 75, 65, ☐, ☐, ☐, 25

4 Here is an arrow.

Now look at these arrows.

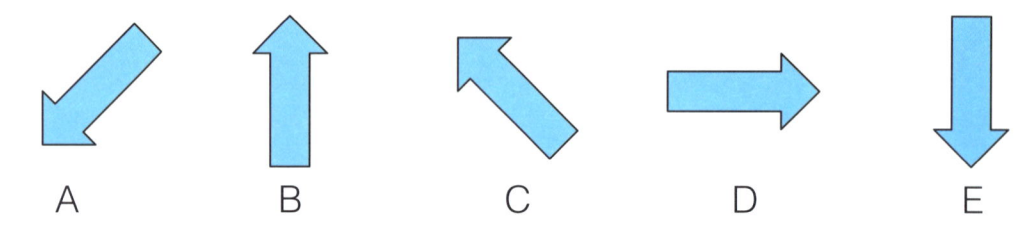

A   B   C   D   E

a Which of these arrows has been turned through one right angle?

1

Q4a

....

b Which has been turned through two right angles?

1

Q4b

....

Letts

5 Here are two shapes.

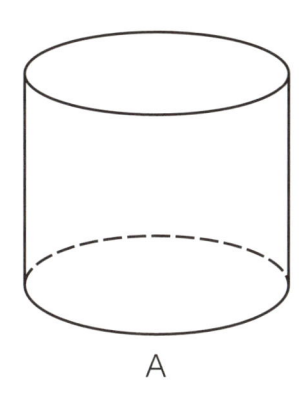 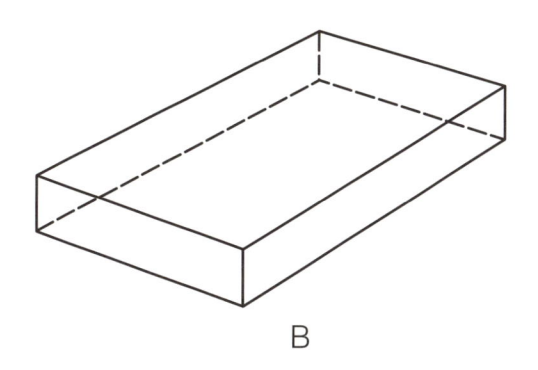

A   B

Here is a list of shape names:

cube   cylinder   pyramid   cuboid   cone

a | What do we call shapes A and B?

2

Q5a

Shape A is a

....

Shape B is a

....

b | Write down **two** differences between them.

2

Q5b

1 ....

2 ....

1

Q6a

1

Q6b

3

Q7

6 Mrs Johnson's class has 33 children in it.

They are going to play a game in teams of 5.

a How many teams will there be?

....

b How many children **cannot** join a team?

....

7 Here is an addition table.

+	10	20	30	100	900
7		27			
15			45		
100					

Fill in the rest of the addition table. Two of the squares have been done for you.

4

8 Look at these shapes.

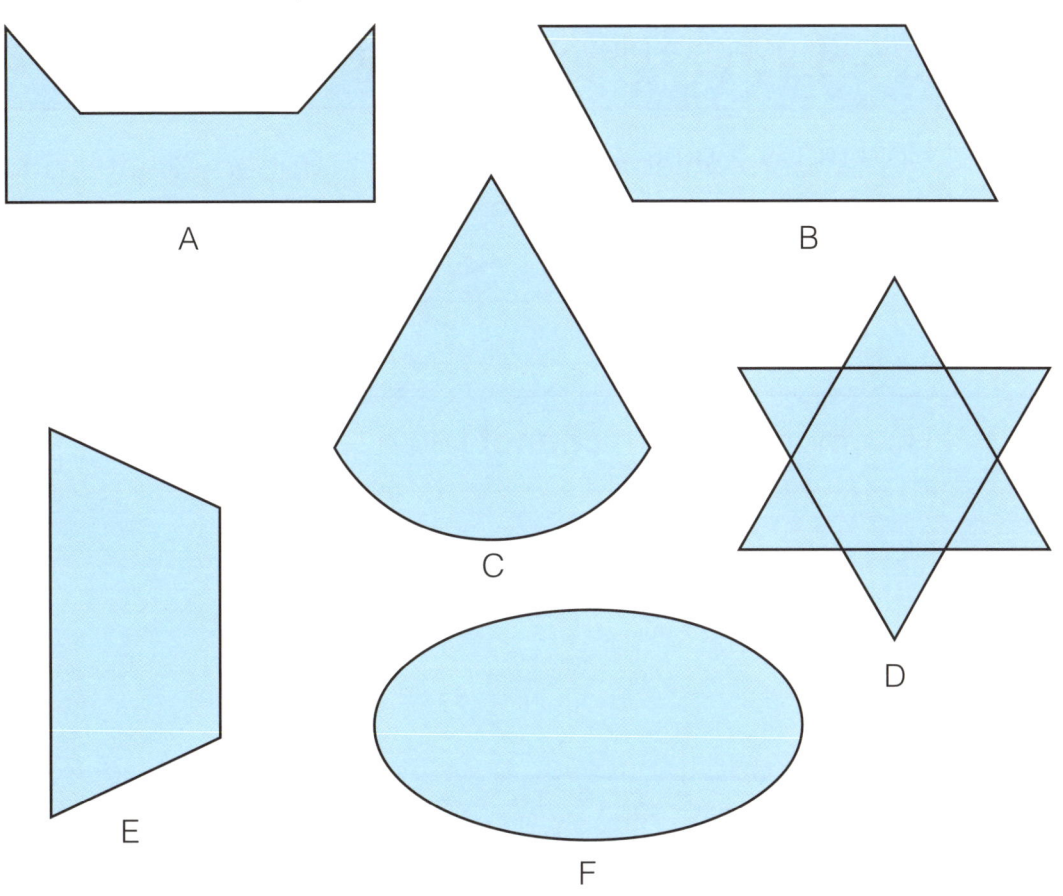

A

B

C

D

E

F

a Which of these shapes have only one line of symmetry?

1

Q8a

....

b Which shapes have more than one line of symmetry?

1

Q8b

....

c Which shapes have no lines of symmetry?

1

Q8c

....

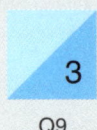
3
Q9

9

Put these numbers in their correct places in the diagram.

| 4 | 6 | 8 | 10 | 20 | 12 | 15 | 5 |

numbers which can be
divided exactly by 2

numbers which can be
divided exactly by 5

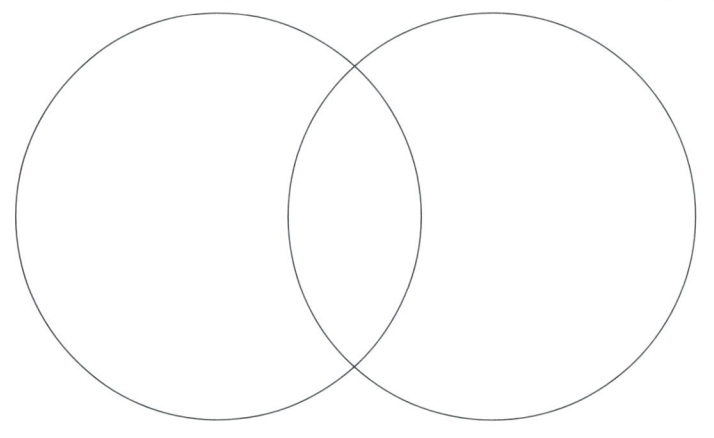

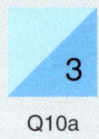
3
Q10a

10 a

Write down the values of:

559 to the nearest 10 ....

136 to the nearest 100 ....

746 to the nearest 100 ....

b

Write down the approximate value of:

103 + 294 + 497

1
Q10b

....

11   Jane is filling containers with water.

1 litre bottle   ½ litre jug   5 litre bucket   100 litre tank

a   How many jugs of water does she need to fill the bottle?

Q11a

b   How many bottles of water does she need to fill the bucket?

Q11b

c   How many buckets of water does she need to fill the tank?

Q11c

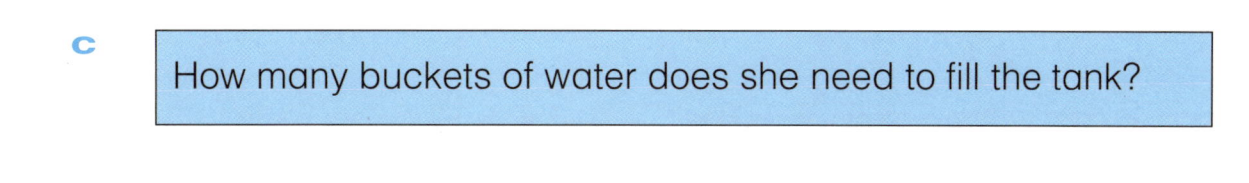

12 Ben measured the height of his family.

Name	Height
Jane	45 cm
Ben	150 cm
Mum	170 cm
Dad	175 cm
Grandma	162 cm
Grandad	180 cm

a Who is the tallest?

1
Q12a

b What is the difference in height between the tallest and the shortest?

1
Q12b

13 A box contains 24 packets of crisps.
Mrs Brown buys a box for £1.28.
She then sells each packet of crisps for 11p per packet.

a How much money does she get?

1
Q13a

b How much profit does she make?

1
Q13b

14 Peter buys a large bar of chocolate which has eight pieces.

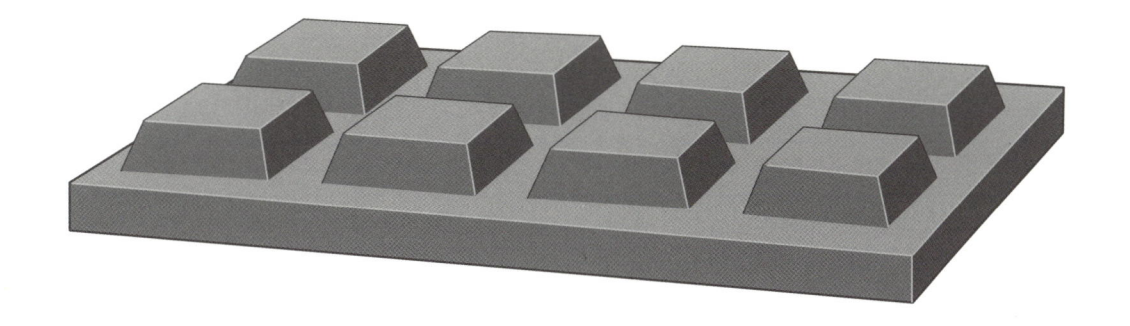

He gives two pieces to George.

a What fraction of his bar has he given to George?

1

Q14a

....

b What fraction does he have left?

1

Q14b

....

Peter then gives four pieces to Jim.

c What fraction of **the whole bar** has he given to Jim?

1

Q14c

....

d What fraction of **the whole bar** does he have left?

1

Q14d

....

9

15 Three men went fishing. This is what they caught.

	Paul	Adam	Richard	Total
Plaice	2	2	0	4
Cod	1	0	2	3
Mackerel	1	3	7	11
Whiting	4	1	0	5

a

1
Q15a

Who caught the most fish?

....

b

1
Q15b

Complete the pictogram showing fish caught by **Paul.**

Plaice     =1 fish

Cod

Mackerel

Whiting

c

1
Q15c

Draw a bar graph showing the total number of fish caught.

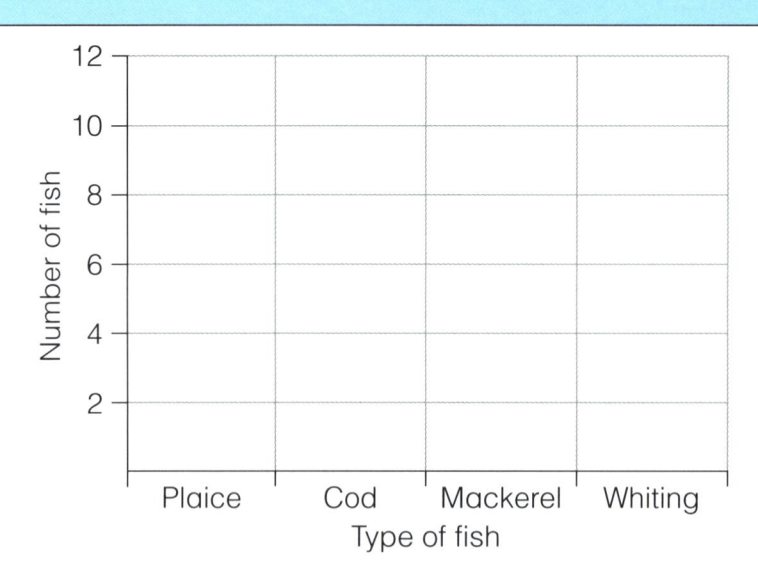

16 This table shows how many children went swimming in one week.

Monday	109
Tuesday	220
Wednesday	171
Thursday	146
Friday	189
Saturday	247

a Write the numbers in order, putting the smallest first.

1
Q16a

....

b What is the difference between the biggest and the smallest number?

1
Q16b

....

c How many more children went swimming on Tuesday than on Wednesday?

1
Q16c

....

On Sunday, 69 more children went swimming than on Thursday.

d How many children went swimming on Sunday?

1
Q16d

....

e How many children went swimming during the seven days?

1
Q16e

....

MARKS

3

Q17

17 Write these percentages in the correct boxes.

20%   50%   9%   30%   40%   75%   60%

Less than a half ($\frac{1}{2}$)	Same as a half ($\frac{1}{2}$)	More than a half ($\frac{1}{2}$)

1

Q18a

18 a Write down the next **two** numbers in this sequence.

   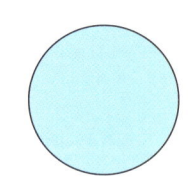

22   24   26

1

Q18b

b Write down the missing numbers in this sequence:

11   21   31

19 Molly has three cards. One with 4 written on it, one with 7 and one with 3.

She moves the cards around to make different three figure numbers like this:

3 4 7

4 7 3

4 3 7

a What is the smallest three figure number she can make?

1

Q19a

b What is the largest three figure number she can make?

1

Q19b

Put the smallest number into your calculator, and use the calculator to add 10.

c What number does your calculator show?

1

Q19c

Put the largest number into your calculator, and use the calculator to multiply by 10.

d What number does the calculator show?

1

Q19d

QUESTIONS
LEVEL 4

20 Tim and Alice were talking about measuring lengths and distances.

a

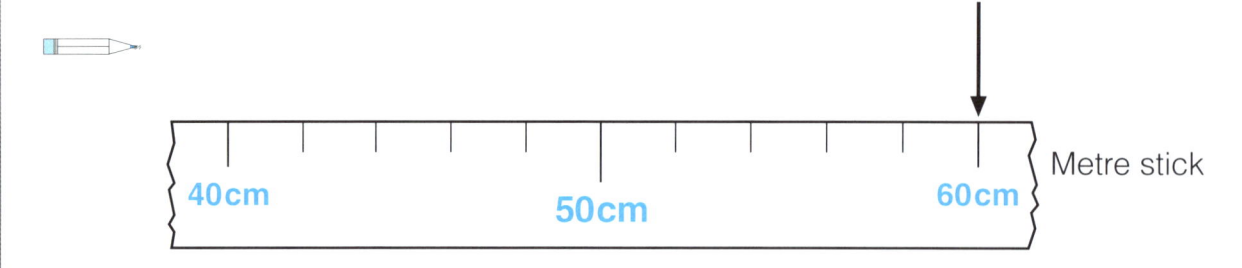

Write down the best unit of measure in the table using words from the list below.

6

Q20a

kilometres   metres   centimetres   millimetres

Distance	Unit
Length of a book	
Distance between two towns	
Length of a classroom	
Width of the school yard	
Height of a child	
Length of a flea	

The children then decide to use a metre stick to take measurements around the school. The arrow on the drawing below shows 60 cm on the metre stick.

40cm   50cm   60cm   Metre stick

b

Draw **two** more arrows to show 58 cm and 45 cm on the metre stick.

2

Q20b

21 Amy and Alex use their calculators to find some large numbers.

Amy

7005

Alex

6998

They want to find the **difference** between these two numbers.

Amy decided to do this by adding:

6998 + 2 = 7000
add 5   = 7005

The difference is 7

Help Amy and Alex to solve these:

3

Q21

a

5006 – 4999

b

6010 – 5991

 4999 + ☐ = 5000

add ☐ = 5006

The difference is ☐

5991 + ☐ = ☐

add ☐ = 6010

The difference is ☐

c

8009 – 7993

 7993 + ☐ = ☐

add ☐ = ☐

The difference is 16

MARKS

22   In my pocket I have:

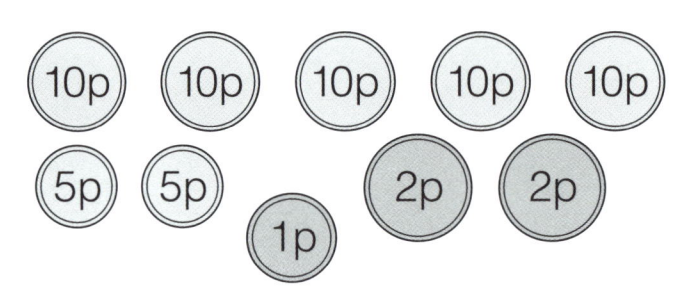

If I draw out one coin at random, how likely is it that I get the following? Tick ✓ **one** box for each question.

	No chance	Poor chance	Even chance	Good chance	Certain
a A 10p coin	☐	☐	☐	☐	☐
b A 2p coin	☐	☐	☐	☐	☐
c A 50p coin	☐	☐	☐	☐	☐

23   Complete these snake number patterns. Fill in the numbers on each snake's body.

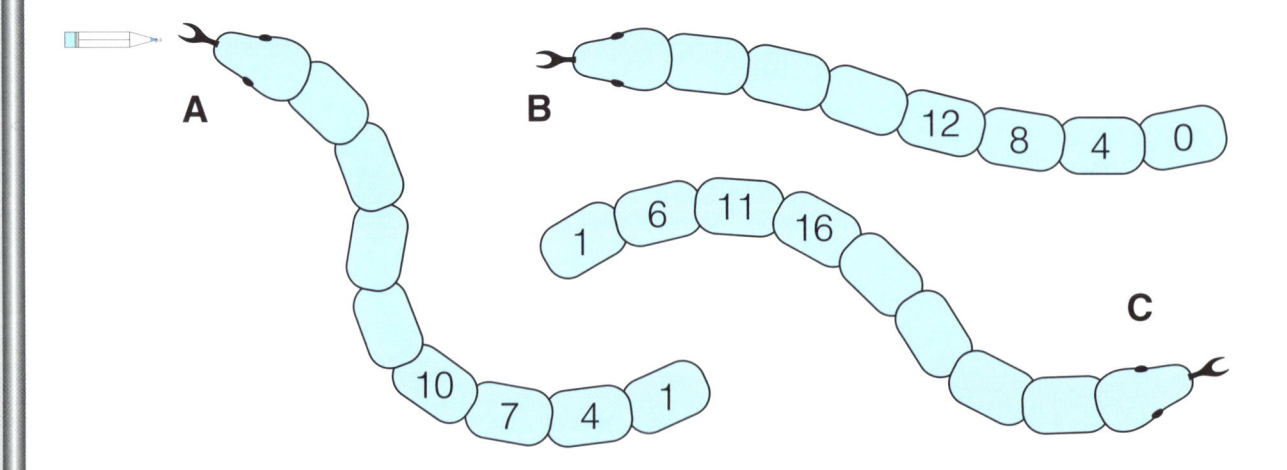

Letts

24 Eleanor has made this picture with Fuzzy-Felts. It has four pairs of congruent shapes in it.

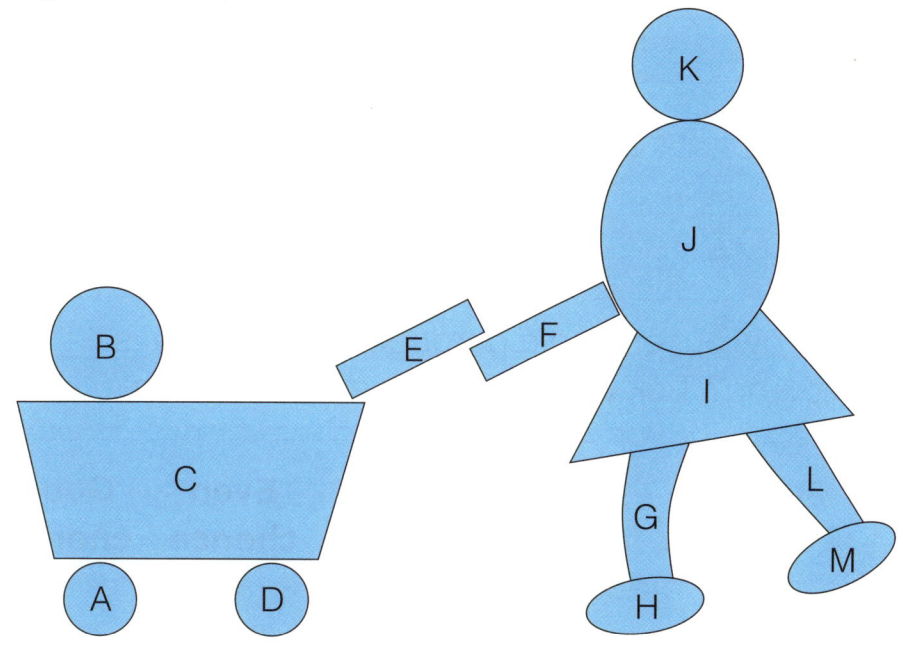

a Can you find the pairs? You may use tracing paper.

Pair 1 is shape .... and shape ....

Pair 2 is shape .... and shape ....

Pair 3 is shape .... and shape ....

Pair 4 is shape .... and shape ....

4
Q24a

b Name the shapes B and E.

Shape B is a ....

Shape E is a ....

2
Q24b

17

25 The graph below shows how much a person's breathing speeds up after running round a track.

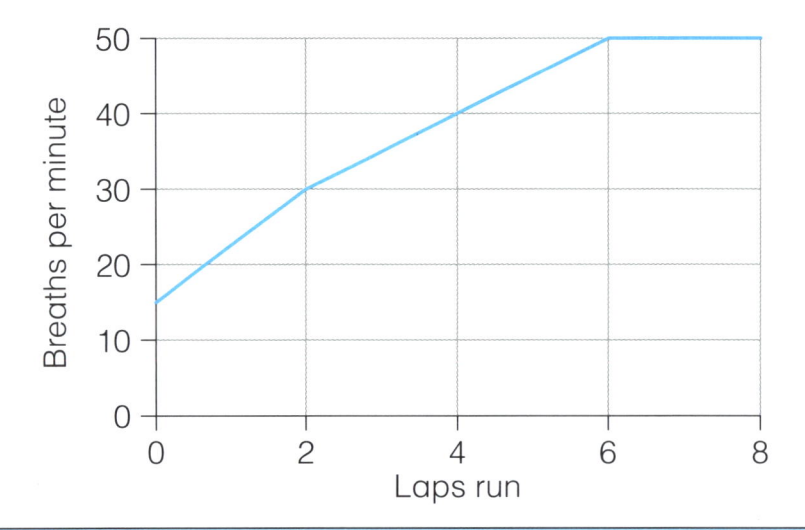

1
Q25a

a How many breaths per minute were taken after running four laps?

✏ ....

1
Q25b

b How many breaths per minute were taken before running round the track?

✏ ....

1
Q25c

c If someone ran seven laps, what would their breathing rate be?

✏ ....

1
Q25d

d How many laps had been run when the rate was 35 breaths per minute?

✏ ....

26 Asif decided to note the prices that garages were charging for 1 litre of petrol.

Here are the prices he wrote down in his notebook

53.1p
52.7p
52.5p
52.9p
52.5p
53.0p
51.9p

a What was the cost of the cheapest petrol?

 ....

Q26a `1`

b What was the cost of the most expensive petrol?

 ....

Q26b `1`

c What was the median cost of the petrol?

 ....

Q26c `1`

27 Jonathon builds this castle using wooden cubes. There is no hole in the middle.

How many cubes did he use?

 ....

Q27 `1`

28 Sharon and Susan are doing a sponsored skip. Both are sponsored for each 5 minutes they can skip.

Susan skips for 40 minutes.

a

> How many 5 minutes are there in 40 minutes?

Daniel sponsors Susan 14p for each 5 minutes.

b

> How much does Daniel pay Susan?

Sharon skips for 1 hour 20 minutes.
Dave sponsors Sharon 8p for each 5 minutes.

c

> How much does Dave pay Sharon?

29

> Match the addition and subtraction sums to the correct answers. The first one has been done for you.

2.43 + 4.14	1.06
4.72 – 1.72	6.57
5.23 + 4.17	9.47
7.11 – 6.05	3.00
8.00 – 6.91	9.40
7.28 + 2.19	1.09

30 a

Plot these co-ordinates, then join them up to make a shape.

(4,4)   (7,4)   (4,1)   (1,1)

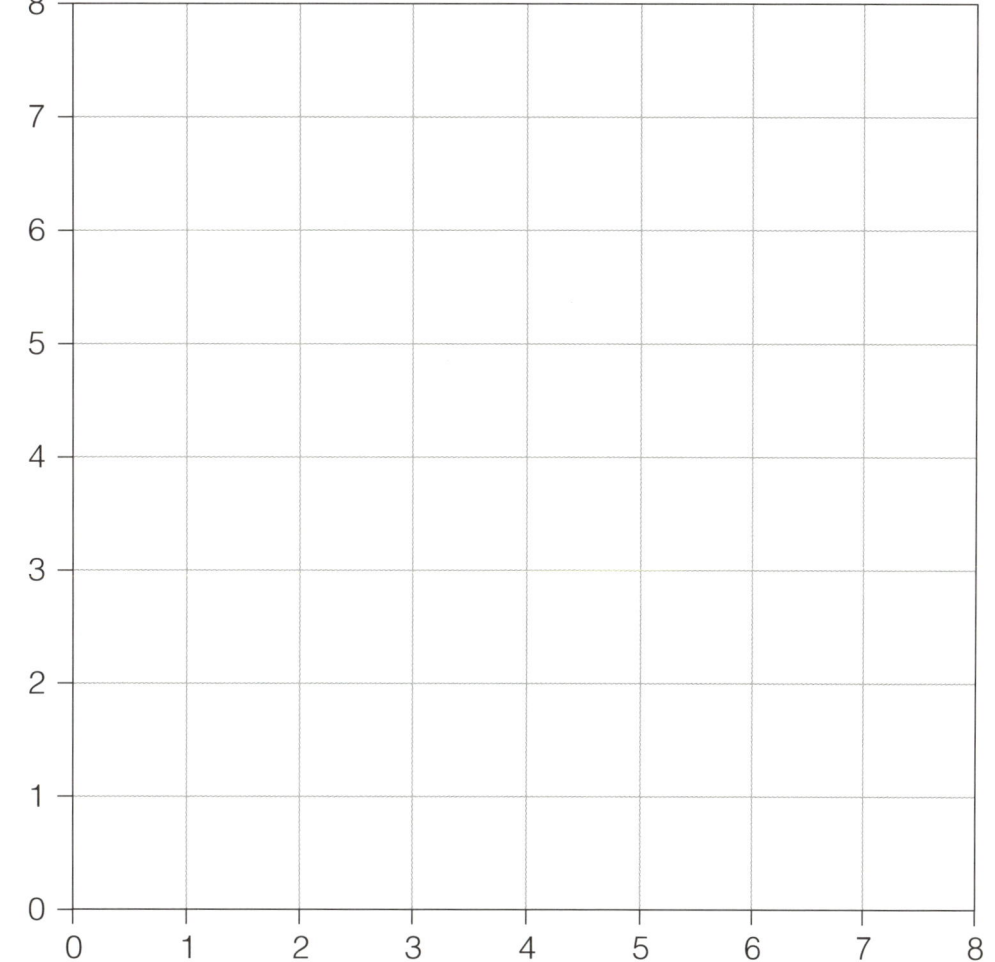

1

Q30a

b

What is the shape called?

1

Q30b

....

c

Find its area.

2

Q30c

....

Letts

31

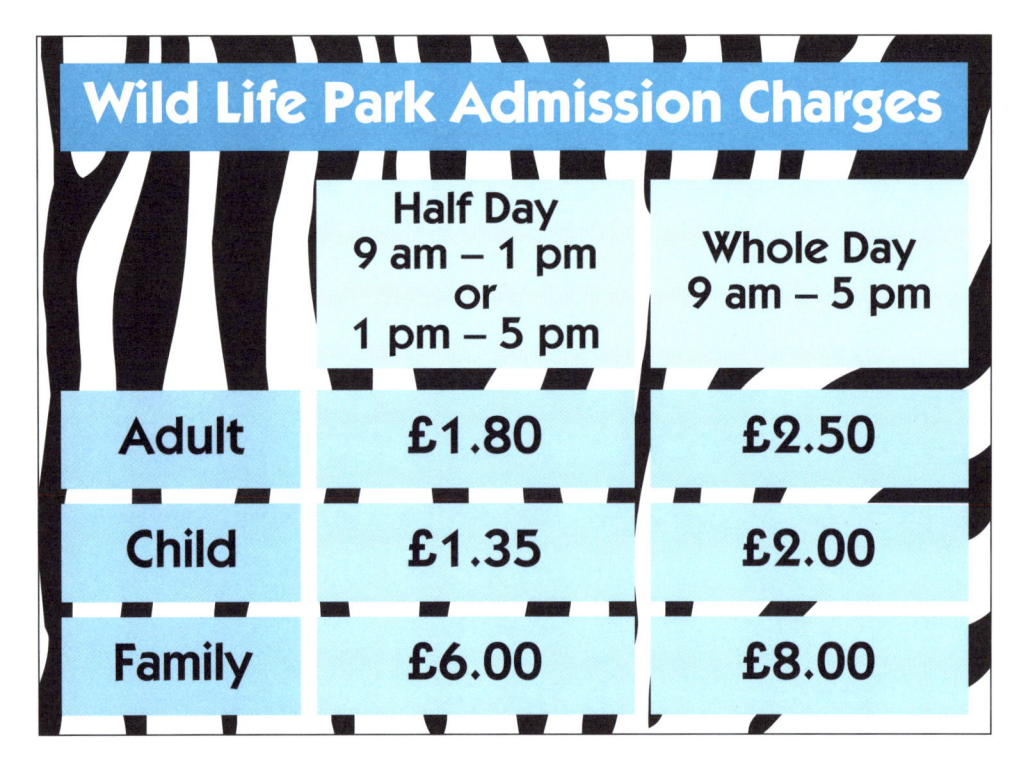

Wild Life Park Admission Charges

	Half Day 9 am – 1 pm or 1 pm – 5 pm	Whole Day 9 am – 5 pm
Adult	£1.80	£2.50
Child	£1.35	£2.00
Family	£6.00	£8.00

The Jones family contains two adults and two children.

a If they just visit for half a day, how much do they save by buying a family ticket?

1

Q31a

....

b How much does it cost **each hour** for the whole family to be there if they buy a half day family ticket?

1

Q31b

....

c If the family buys a whole day family ticket and spent the day there, how much does each hour of their visit cost them then?

1

Q31c

....

Letts

32 Jane and Ahmed are drawing shapes on the computer screen.
Jane plots the following points: (1, 3) (1, 7) (4, 7) (5, 5) (1, 3)
Ahmed plots these points: (5, 4) (9, 4) (9, 2) (6, 1) (5, 4)
The computer joins up the points with straight lines.

a Draw both shapes using Jane's and Ahmed's co-ordinates.

2

Q32a

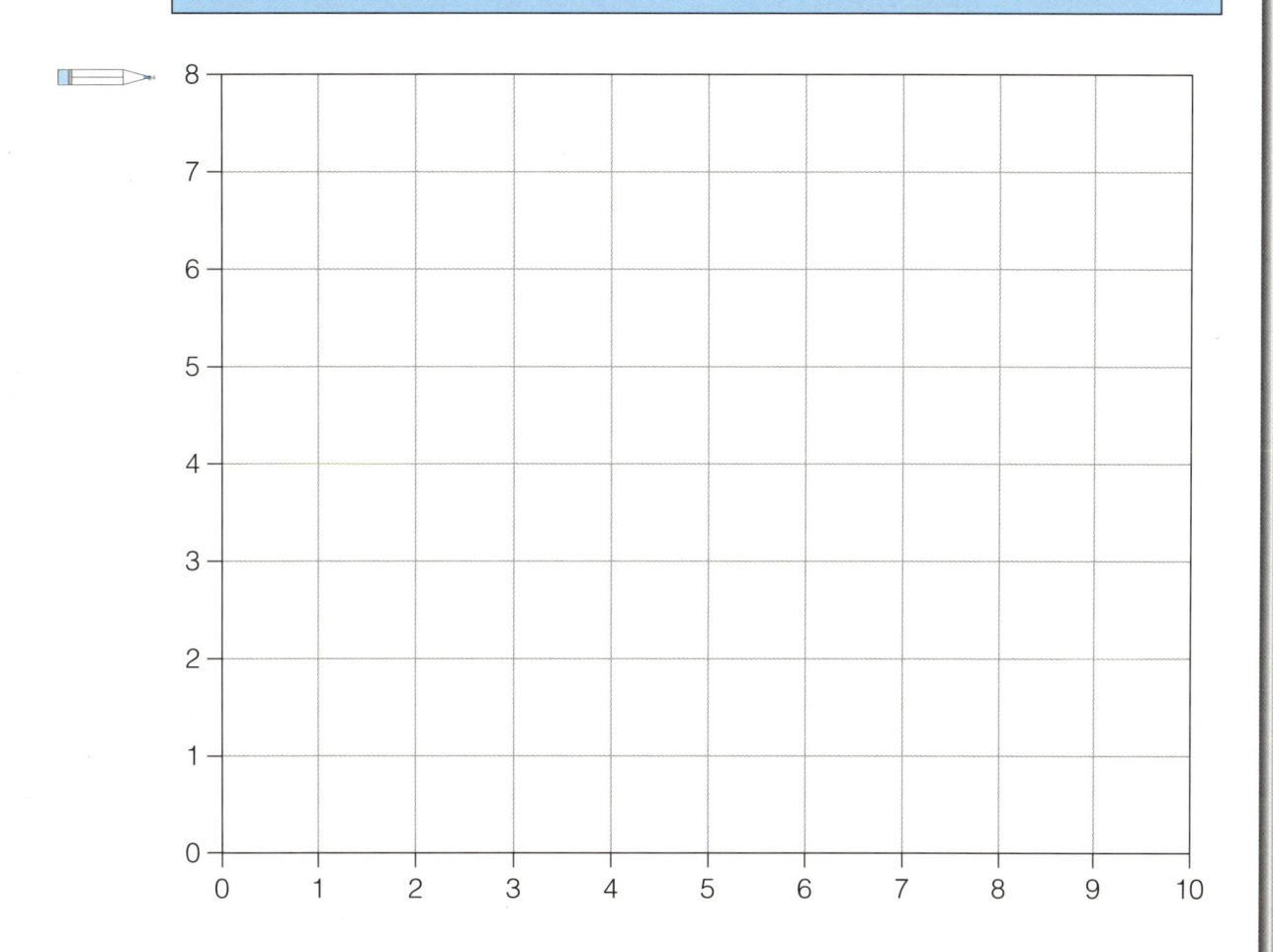

b Find **three** things that are the same about both shapes.

3

Q32b

1 ....

2 ....

3 ....

23

33 Look at this thermometer.

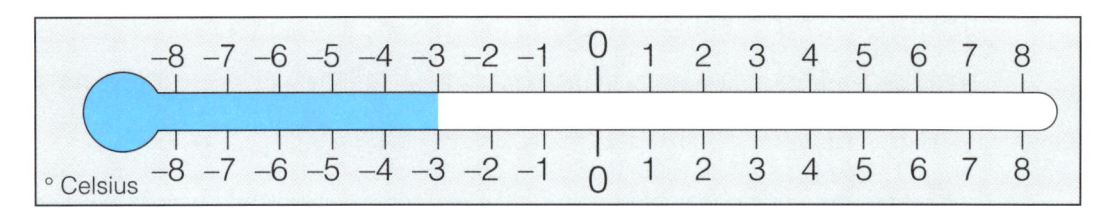

a What temperature is shown on the thermometer?

b Work out the finishing temperatures column on this table.

Starting temperature	Change of temperature	Finishing temperature
0°C	5°C colder	
−4°C	5°C warmer	
2°C	6°C colder	
−3°C	2°C colder	

34 John, Joe and Jeremy weed Mrs Roberts garden. She gives them £10 to share equally.

a How much does each one get?

b How much will be left over?

35

During a sale, Mr. Patel reduced the price of his choco bars by half.

a | How much would each choco bar cost in the sale?

1

Q35a

....

He reduces the price of his brushes by one third.

b | How much would you save?

1

Q35b

....

The packets of stickers are reduced as well. He takes a quarter off their price.

c | What is the sale price of a packet of stickers?

1

Q35c

....

Letts

36 Sarah's family are preparing for a camping holiday. Sarah packs three bags for their first day's food.

Bag 1

Breakfast

Tin of tomatoes	375g
Packet of cereal	500g
Sausages	900g

Bag 2

Lunch

Sandwiches	400g
Cans of drink	500g

Bag 3

Evening Meal

Potatoes	1200g
Burgers	400g
Tin of soup	375g

3

Q36a

a How much does each bag weigh in grams?

Bag 1 ....

Bag 2 ....

Bag 3 ....

3

Q36b

b How much does each bag weigh in kilograms?

Bag 1 ....

Bag 2 ....

Bag 3 ....

1

Q36c

c Which **two** items have a total weight of 1.3 kg?

....

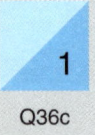

37   Hayley is making a pattern using pegs and a peg board. She wants the pattern to have symmetry.

a

Draw in the line of symmetry. (The left hand side is already complete.

Q37a

b

Complete the pattern to make it symmetrical.

Q37b

38 Mr Davy the greengrocer buys boxes of apples for £6.

He sells each box for 30% more.

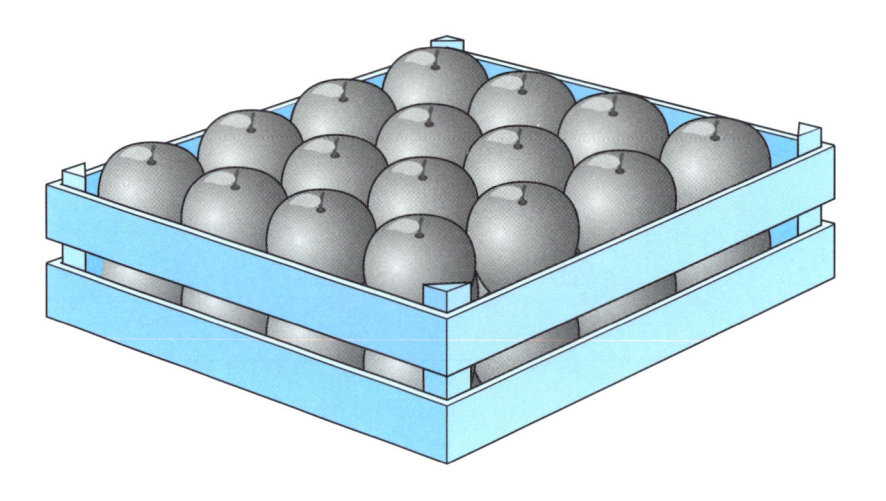

a

| How much is the selling price? |

He bought ten of these boxes, but was given a reduction of 20% for bulk buying.

b

| How much did he pay for the ten boxes? |

He finds that 5% of the apples are rotten.

c

| If the total weight of apples he bought is 40kg, what weight of apples is all right to eat? |

39 Elliott has four cards.

| 9 | 3 | 1 | . |

One has a 9 written on, one has a 3, one has a 1 and the last has a decimal point.

Elliott uses these cards to make different numbers each with **one** decimal figure, for example:

| 1 | 9 | . | 3 | | 3 | 9 | . | 1 |

a What is the smallest number he can make with all four cards?

1

Q39a

....

b What is the largest number he can make?

1

Q39b

....

Put the smallest number into your calculator. Use your calculator to add 10 to this number.

c What figures does your calculator show?

1

Q39c

....

Put the largest number into your calculator. Use your calculator to divide by 10.

d What figure does your calculator show?

1

Q39d

....

Letts

40 Stephen bought a bag with ten packets of toffees in.

He counted the number of toffees in each packet.

Here are his results.

16, 18, 15, 16, 17, 14, 16, 14, 16, 15

a What is the modal number of toffees in a packet?

....

b Work out the median number of toffees in a packet.

....

c Work out the mean number of toffees in a packet.

....

Stephen says the average number of toffees is 16.

d Do you agree with him? Explain why.

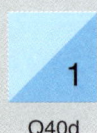

....

....

41 Choose the most suitable number from the list to complete these sentences.

6

Q41

2   5   10   15   25   75   200   250   500

a  The weight of an egg is about .... g.

b  The time taken for Linford Christie to run the 100 m is about .... seconds.

c  The height of a door is about .... m

d  The capacity of a mug is about .... ml.

e  The length of a pencil is about .... cm.

f 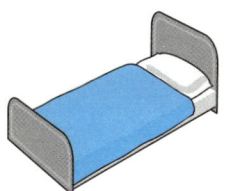 The length of a bed is about .... cm.

Letts

42   Mrs Smith's class had the following lunches at school one day.

Hot dinner	15
Salad	3
Sandwiches	12

a   One child is picked at random. What is the probability that he had a hot dinner? Mark it on the probability line.

0   1

b   Explain how you decided.

....

....

c   What is the probability that one of the class, chosen at random had sandwiches?

....

MARKING YOUR CHILD'S QUESTIONS

- The answers given here are correct answers. They are the answers the question-setter expects. When marking your child's questions, you must look at your child's answers and judge whether they deserve credit. Award the mark if the answer deserves credit.

- At this age, your child's spelling may show a number of errors. Do not mark any answer wrong because the words are misspelt. Read the word aloud and if it sounds correct award the mark. For example, 'ekwul' would be acceptable for 'equal'.

- When you go through the questions with your child, try to be positive. Look for good things that have been done in addition to showing where errors have been made.

- Enter your child's marks on the grid on page 46, and then refer to the chart below to determine your child's level.

Progress Chart

Total marks scored	Progress made	Suggested action
20 or below	Your child still needs help and support to be confident with work at Level 2.	Try to identify difficulties in the early questions, particularly the first five. Work through them with your child and use the notes to help.
21–50	Your child is working with confidence within Level 3.	Practise questions using addition and subtraction, the multiplication tables and measurement.
51–80	Your child is working with growing confidence within Level 4.	The multiplication tables (up to 10×10) should be known; questions involving simple fractions and percentages could be practised.
81–110	Your child is reasonably confident with the Level 4 work presented here.	Practise questions involving area, perimeter, median and mode.
111 or above	Your child is working with increasing confidence within Level 5.	A good score, but keep practising questions with two decimal places and those involving the mean.

- A child at the end of Year 5 (9–10 year olds) should be, of the above statements, at about the third statement.

1 Any four answers from:
0 + 4,   1 + 3,   2 + 2,   1 + 1 + 2,   1 + 1 + 1 + 1   *1 mark each*

Note to Parent

This question can be extended. It is useful to encourage your child to write down the different ways systematically.

Total 4 marks

2 a   21   *1 mark*
    b   42p   *1 mark*

Note to Parent

This is a typical example of the sort of straight forward question that is useful to give your child practice. It is fairly easy to make up other similar questions.

Total 2 marks

3 a   33 36 37   *1 mark*
    b   55 45 35   *1 mark*

Note to Parent

Ask your child to talk about the sequences and the patterns. In **a** your child ought to explain that the numbers go up in ones. In **b** that the numbers are going down in tens, or that the last digit is five etc.

Total 2 marks

4 a   D   *1 mark*
    b   E   *1 mark*

Note to Parent

Encourage your child to recognise right angle turns and right angles around the house etc.

Total 2 marks

5 a   shape A is a cylinder, shape B is a cuboid   *1 mark each*
    b   A has circular ends   B has rectangular ends
        A has curved faces   B has flat faces
        A has no corners   B has eight corners
        A has three faces   B has six faces
        Any two answers, one mark each   *2 marks*

Note to Parent

Ask your child to describe the differences between other regular objects that you might see.

Total 4 marks

6 a 6 *1 mark*
 b 3 *1 mark*

Note to Parent

If your child has difficulty in visualising how many groups of 5 there are in 33, it may help to use counters etc.

Total 2 marks

7

17		37	107	907
25	35		115	915
110	120	130	200	1000

Award three marks if all are correct; two marks if there is one error;
one mark if two errors; no marks if more than two errors *3 marks*

Note to Parent

Number patterns are not much help here! If this proves difficult for your child, it might help her or him to use a diagram with hundreds, tens and units as column headings.

Total 3 marks

8 a A, C, E *1 mark*
 b D, F *1 mark*
 c B *1 mark*

Note to Parent

Your child may use a mirror to help him or her identify shapes that have reflection symmetry.

Total 3 marks

9

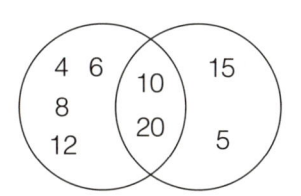

Award one mark for each section correctly completed *3 marks*

Note to Parent

Sorting into appropriate categories is an important basic skill for data handling. Note the 'overlap' in this example.

Total 3 marks

10 a   560   *1 mark*
             100   *1 mark*
             700   *1 mark*
    b   100 + 300 + 500 = 900   *1 mark*

Note to Parent

If your child found the answers to the last part of **a** was 800 he or she probably rounded to the nearest 10 first (i.e. 750) and then to the nearest 100. This is wrong because 746 is nearer to 700 than 800. In **b** the numbers should be approximated first and then added (see answer above).

Total 4 marks

11 a   2   *1 mark*
    b   5   *1 mark*
    c   20   *1 mark*

Note to Parent

As with most measurement questions, practical experience of capacity is a must for proper understanding to take place. Children need to fill and empty containers, working with litres and millilitres. Everyday household objects will usually be all that is required, for example medicine spoons, shampoo bottles and kitchen measuring jugs. A comparison between litres and pints (using milk bottles and milk cartons) will also provide children with comparisons of imperial and metric measures.

Total 3 marks

12 a   Grandad   *1 mark*
    b   135cm or 1m 35cm   *1 mark*

Note to Parent

Children need to be able to interpret values in tables and then to calculate with those values. This is a simple question to test those skills.

Total 2 marks

13 a   £2.64   *1 mark*
    b   £2.64 – £1.28 = £1.36   *1 mark*

Note to Parent

This question can be answered using a calculator. Encourage your child to be consistent – either work in pounds throughout, so that 11 pence would be entered as 0.11, or work in pence and then divide by 100.

Total 2 marks

14 a ¼ (allow ⅜)   *1 mark*
        b ¾ (allow ⁶⁄₈)   *1 mark*
        c ½ (allow ⁴⁄₈)   *1 mark*
        d ¼ (allow ⅜)   *1 mark*

Note to Parent

Use a chocolate bar as an aid, or use a piece of folded paper and write in the fraction of the shape like this:

| ½ | ½ |

| ¼ | ¼ |
| ¼ | ¼ |

Total 4 marks

15 a Richard   *1 mark*

        b Plaice   🐟 🐟
           Cod   🐟
           Mackerel 🐟
           Whiting   🐟 🐟 🐟 🐟   *1 mark*

        c 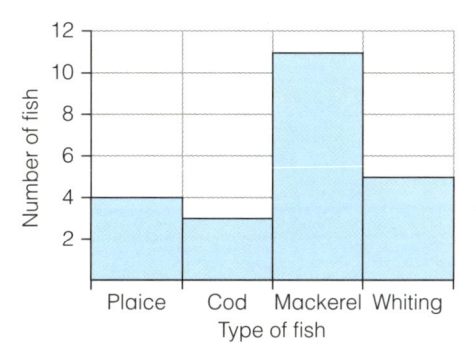   *1 mark*

Note to Parent

Children need to be able to construct pictograms and simple graphs.

Total 3 marks

16 a 109, 146, 171, 189, 220, 247   *1 mark*
        b 138   *1 mark*
        c 49   *1 mark*
        d 215   *1 mark*
        e 1297   *1 mark*

Note to Parent

Your child will probably find a calculator useful for this question. The word 'more' in parts **c** and **d** may need explaining.

Total 5 marks

17

Less than half	Same as a half	More than a half
20%	50%	60%
9%		75%
30%		
40%		

Award one mark for each correctly completed box   *3 marks*

> **Note to Parent**
>
> Children are meant to know the equivalence of fractions and percentages at a later stage. This question tests the comparison of a percentage with a familiar fraction, such as one half.

Total 3 marks

18 a   28 30   *1 mark*
      b   16 26   *1 mark*

> **Note to Parent**
>
> This question looks at sequencing numbers. In **b** the answer is found by thinking of the number halfway between 11 and 21 and between 21 and 31.

Total 2 marks

19 a   smallest 347   *1 mark*
      b   largest 743   *1 mark*
      c   357   *1 mark*
      d   7430   *1 mark*

> **Note to Parent**
>
> Children have to be confident with using calculators and with place value. This question tests both. Use actual cards with numbers on if it helps.

Total 4 marks

20 a   book – centimetres   *1 mark*
          towns – kilometres   *1 mark*
          classroom – metres   *1 mark*
          school yard – metres   *1 mark*
          child – centimetres   *1 mark*
          flea – millimetres   *1 mark*

> **Note to Parent**
>
> Although it is possible to measure any of these lengths using any of the units given, the best possible solutions are provided in the answers. The height of a child could also be given in metres, but decimal notation would probably be required and would not be appropriate for some children at this age.

b

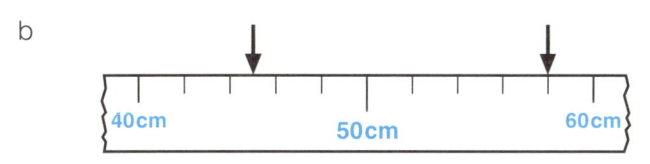

Award one mark for each arrow 2 marks

Note to Parent

Early experience of measurement involves relations and comparisons between objects, for example larger, taller, smallest. Leading on from this, children are introduced to measurement units which can be both non-standard and standard. An example of a non-standard unit would be a hand span which would obviously vary from person to person. Standard units are those that have been agreed on internationally, for example the metre. This question tests your child's understanding of common metric units of length and provides contexts in which only some units would be appropriate to use.

Total 8 marks

21 a 4999 + 1 = 5000 add 6 = 5006 Difference is 7 *1 mark*

b 5991 + 9 = 6000 add 10 = 6010 Difference is 19 *1 mark*

c 7993 + 7 = 8000 add 9 = 8009

*There are other solutions to **c**, but the difference will be 16* *1 mark*

Note to Parent

At first sight these questions may seem strange and somewhat laboured. Children are meant to have a range of mental strategies for dealing with the four operations of addition, subtraction, multiplication and division. These questions are attempting to assess your child's competence with these strategies – they mirror the way people might work out the answers mentally.

Total 3 marks

22 a Even chance *1 mark*

b Poor chance *1 mark*

c No chance *1 mark*

Note to Parent

Children do not need to work out precisely the odds to answer a question like this, but it is typical of the sort of question one might use to get them started on doing so. In part **a** there are five out of ten chances of getting a 10p coin, so it is an even chance. In **b** there are two out of ten chances of a 2p coin, so it is a poor chance. In **c** there is no 50p coin, so there is no chance.

The language of probability is varied. The word 'chance' is in common everday use, but your child may have met the words impossible (no chance), unlikely (poor chance) and likely (between an even chance and certain).

Total 3 marks

23   A   13   16   19   22   *1 mark*
      B   16   20   24   *1 mark*
      C   21   26   31   36   *1 mark*

Note to Parent

Encourage your child to look for patterns and to talk about the patterns they see, for example 'The numbers go up in threes'. Use a number line or a tape measure marked in centimetres to help.

Total 3 marks

24   a   The pairs, in any order, are:
          B and K, H and M, E and F, A and D
          Award one mark for each correct pair   *4 marks*
      b   Shape B is a circle   *1 mark*
          Shape E is a rectangle   *1 mark*

Note to Parent

Congruent shapes are identical. Tracing paper is used to check.

Total 6 marks

25   a   40   *1 mark*
      b   15   *1 mark*
      c   50   *1 mark*
      d   3   *1 mark*

Note to Parent

If it helps, suggest to your child that she or he draws a line up the page through four laps and then across the page to read the breaths per minute. Note that in part **d** the process is reversed – the value on the axis up the page is used to read across and down to the axis across the page.

Total 4 marks

26   a   51.9p   *1 mark*
      b   53.1p   *1 mark*
      c   52.7p   *1 mark*

Note to Parent

The median value is the middle value. The values (here prices) should be arranged in order, smallest to largest. The median is the middle number if the number of values in the list is odd, and is halfway between the two middle numbers if the number of values is even.

Total 3 marks

27   72 cubes   *1 mark*

Note to Parent

Your child should solve this problem by realising there are 4 × 4 = 16 cubes on the bottom layer. There are four layers, that is 16 + 16 + 16 + 16, plus 8 cubes for the towers.

Total 1 mark

28 a   8   *1 mark*
    b   £1.12 *or* 112p   *1 mark*
    c   £1.28 *or* 128p   *2 marks*

Note to Parent

This question tests some basic mathematics in a different context, for example 40 minutes divided by 5 minutes. For part **c**, encourage your child to treat it as a two-part question – first find how many 5 minutes there are in 1 hour 20 minutes, then multiply that answer by 8. Award one mark for each correct part.

Total 4 marks

29 4.72 – 1.72 = 3.00   *1 mark*
    5.23 + 4.17 = 9.40   *1 mark*
    7.11 – 6.05 = 1.06   *1 mark*
    8.00 – 6.91 = 1.09   *1 mark*
    7.28 + 2.19 = 9.47   *1 mark*

Note to Parent

Although this question can be answered using a calculator, encourage your child to reason mentally and to calculate mentally as much as possible, for example:
7.28 + 2.19 must be over 9 because 7 + 2 = 9
and it must end in 7 because 8 + 9 = 17.
Then check with a calculator.

Total 5 marks

30 a

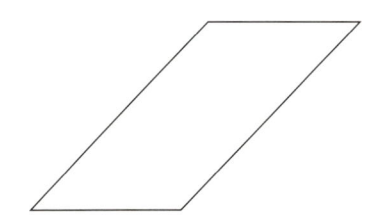

    Award one mark for correctly plotting and drawing the shape   *1 mark*
    b   parallelogram   *1 mark*
    c   9 square units   *2 marks*

Note to Parent

This activity encourages your child to plot co-ordinates on a grid. Make sure they know that the first number in each pair is the distance across the grid and the second number is the distance up the grid. Part **c** will need to be done by counting squares and half squares.

Total 4 marks

31 a   30p or £0.30   *1 mark*
    b   150p or £1.50 an hour   *1 mark*
    c   100p or £1.00 an hour   *1 mark*

Note to Parent

Children need to be able to extract and interpret information from everyday examples.

Total 3 marks

32 a

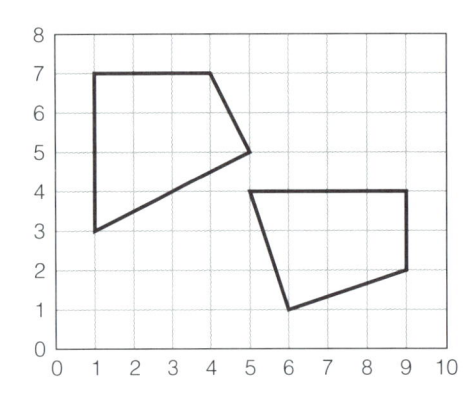

Award one mark for each correctly drawn shape   *2 marks*

b   Similar features include:
both shapes have four sides (quadrilaterals)
both have straight edges
both contain a right angle
none of their sides are equal
Award one mark for each correct statement   *3 marks*

Note to Parent

The first number of each pair of co-ordinates gives the distance across the grid, and the second number the distance up the grid.

Total 5 marks

33 a   –3°C   *1 mark*

b   Finishing temperatures:
–5°C   *1 mark*
1°C   *1 mark*
–4°C   *1 mark*
–5°C   *1 mark*

Note to Parent

Your child needs to understand that once the temperature drops below 0°C, the temperature becomes a minus number. The drawing of the thermometer at the top of the page may be used to help with part **b**.

Total 5 marks

34 a   10 ÷ 3 = £3.33 to the nearest penny   *1 mark*
b   £3.33 × 3 = £9.99 so 1p is left over   *1 mark*

Note to Parent

This question tests your child's ability to interpret the calculator display. Answers to questions involving money should be given to the nearest penny.

Total 2 marks

35   a   21p   *1 mark*
    b   31p   *1 mark*
    c   57p   *1 mark*

Note to Parent

To complete this activity, your child must realise that to halve a number it is divided into two groups, to find a third into three groups and so on. So, to find the new price of the stickers, for example, find a quarter of 76p (= 19p) and subtract it from 76p. Practising beforehand with counters, coins or pencils may be helpful.

Total 3 marks

36   a   Bag 1   1775 g   *1 mark*
       Bag 2   900 g   *1 mark*
       Bag 3   1975 g   *1 mark*
    b   Bag 1   1.775 kg   *1 mark*
       Bag 2   0.9 kg   *1 mark*
       Bag 3   1.975 kg   *1 mark*
    c   sausages and sandwiches *or* sausages and burgers   *1 mark*

Note to Parent

Measurement of weight (or more accurately mass) involves skills of estimation, reading off scales and knowledge of standard units. This question mainly involves the latter and in particular the relation of grams to kilograms and conversion from one unit to the other. Writing metric measures in different units involves knowledge of place value and decimals. It is useful for children to practise conversion with many examples involving weight, length and capacity. For example:
   675 g = 0.675 kg   1200 m = 1.2 km   42 cm = 0.42 m

Total 7 marks

37

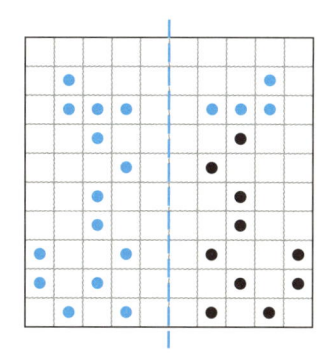

Award one mark for drawing the line of symmetry correctly and one mark for correctly positioning the dots   *2 marks*

Note to Parent

Children are required to both recognise reflective symmetry and also transform (change) shapes by reflection. Work on reflective or line symmetry can best be developed practically with the aid of a small mirror.

Total 2 marks

38 a £7.80
Award one mark for 30% of £6 = £1.80; one mark for £6 + £1.80 *2 marks*

b £48
Award one mark for 20% of £60 = £12; one mark for £60 – £12 *2 marks*

c 38 kg
Award one mark for 5% of 40 kg = 2 kg; one mark for 40 kg – 2 kg *2 marks*

Note to Parent

The usual way of dealing with percentage increases and decreases is to find, for example, 30% of £6 and then add the answer to £6. However it is easier (and quicker) to multiply by: $\left(1 + \dfrac{\% \text{ change}}{100}\right)$.

So in part **a** the answer can be found by:

$1 + \dfrac{30}{100} = 1.3$ multiplied by 6 = $1.3 \times 6 = 7.80$ (£7.80).

In part b:

$10 \times £6 = £60$ a 20% reduction is $1 - \dfrac{20}{100} = 0.8$, therefore $60 \times 0.8 = 48$ (£48)

Total 6 marks

39 a 13.9 *1 mark*
b 93.1 *1 mark*
c 23.9 *1 mark*
d 9.31 *1 mark*

Note to Parent

Children need to know how to multiply (and divide) decimal numbers by 10 (and 100 and 1000). You can extend this question to division and multiplication by 100 and 1000. Some children may find it helpful to actually use cards to answer the first part of this question.

Total 4 marks

40 a 16 *1 mark*
b 16 *1 mark*
c 15.7
Award one mark for the correct total = 157; one mark for dividing by 10 *2 marks*
d Yes. All are 16 to the nearest whole number *1 mark*

Note to Parent

Mode is the value that occurs most often. The median is the middle value when the values are placed in size order: 14, 14, 15, 15, 16, 16, 16, 16, 17, 18. Here there is no single middle value, so to find the median add the two middle values and divide by two (see Note to Parent, question 26). The mean is the average value when all the values are added up and the sum is divided by the number of values. The fact that all three 'averages' have the same value is somewhat unusual.

Total 5 marks

41
a	75 grams		*1 mark*
b	10 seconds		*1 mark*
c	2 metres		*1 mark*
d	250 millilitres		*1 mark*
e	15 cm		*1 mark*
f	200 cm		*1 mark*

Note to Parent

The ability to estimate, approximate and to know approximate values needs developing. Try to think of other questions to ask your child.

Total 6 marks

42
a

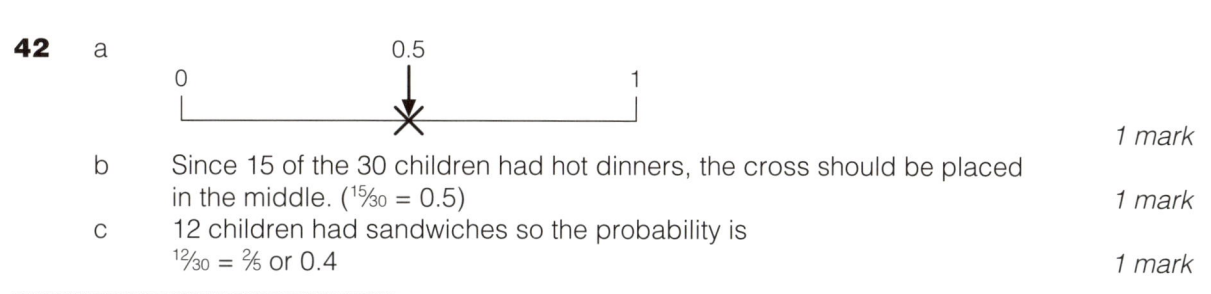

1 mark

b Since 15 of the 30 children had hot dinners, the cross should be placed in the middle. ($^{15}\!/_{30}$ = 0.5) *1 mark*

c 12 children had sandwiches so the probability is
$^{12}\!/_{30}$ = $^2\!/_5$ or 0.4 *1 mark*

Note to Parent

The probabilities are found by dividing the number of children who satisfy the condition by the total number of children.

Total 3 marks

MARKING GRID

Question	Marks available	Marks scored
1	4	
2	2	
3	2	
4	2	
5	4	
Total	**14**	

Question	Marks available	Marks scored
6	2	
7	3	
8	3	
9	3	
10	4	
11	3	
12	2	
13	2	
14	4	
15	3	
16	5	
Total	**34**	

Question	Marks available	Marks scored
17	3	
18	2	
19	4	
20	8	
21	3	
22	3	
23	3	
24	6	
25	4	
26	3	
27	1	
28	4	
29	5	
30	4	
31	3	
32	5	
Total	**61**	

Question	Marks available	Marks scored
33	5	
34	2	
35	3	
36	7	
37	2	
38	6	
39	4	
40	5	
41	6	
42	3	
Total	**43**	